**PARIS
IN FIFTY
DESIGN ICONS**

50

the
DESIGN
MUSEUM

50

PARIS
IN FIFTY
DESIGN ICONS

BRIGITTE
FITOUSSI
& IMOGEN
FORTES

conran
OCTOPUS

# PARIS

# INTRODUCTION

'Paris is a moveable feast…' wrote Ernest Hemingway (1899–1961) who, following the tradition of many artists and writers, had fallen madly in love with the city. Dubbed the 'City of Light', Paris has been at the forefront of the worlds of fashion and luxury ever since, attracting visitors in their millions, interrupted only by tragic attacks (such as those in November 2015) that left it almost deserted.

The city's unique urban landscape owes much to the efforts of French civil servant Baron Georges-Eugène Haussmann (1809–91), whose famous '*Grands Boulevards*' can still be seen today. At its historic centre, however, Paris has preserved the imprint of centuries past in the layout of some of the streets in the Marais or on the Île de la Cité. There are listed buildings as far as the eye can see, and a host of different rulers and leaders have left their mark across the years – a perennial French ambition.

The Right Bank, the Left Bank … Paris would not be Paris without the meandering of its river. Spanned by more than 30 crossings, the oldest of which is paradoxically the 'new bridge', the Pont Neuf, the river Seine carves a particularly romantic path through the city, especially at night. The many admirers who describe Paris as 'the most beautiful city in the world' are gently mocked by Woody Allen in his nostalgic 2011 film *Midnight in Paris*, which was inspired by Hemingway's book. Its critics, on the other hand, dismiss it as an 'inhabited museum', overly elitist and gentrified throughout. While its suburbs, or *banlieue*, were declared the 'Metropolis of Greater Paris' in 2016, this is yet to have any tangible effects.

Nonetheless, with its wealth of urban diversity, unique lifestyle, living spaces, temples of culture and fashion, museums and monuments, Paris manages to pack its 20 very different districts with a veritable anthology of icons. Choosing just 50 is a nightmarish task that highlights the tension between capturing the spirit of the age and notions of permanence. The Eiffel Tower is a monument, symbol and icon in one. The Maison de Verre or the Galerie Kreo, design icons of a different kind, appeal perhaps more to the cognoscenti. Icons, history and fashion are all intimately entangled here. They expose a subjective path illuminated by the bright gleam of a modernity that never truly outshines its past. That's Paris.

Competitors in the Tour de France cycle through the Arc de Triomphe in 1937. The closing stage in Paris is now a highlight of the world's best-known cycling race.

# NOTRE DAME CATHEDRAL
## Our Lady of Paris

Gothic cathedrals were the skyscrapers of their day – buildings of eminent stature, grandeur and visibility – and, thanks to Paris's strict building regulations, which govern the height of new construction in the city, Notre Dame continues to boast these attributes, enjoying a clear sightline from across the city.

The cathedral is the heart of Paris – it stands on the site of Paris's first Christian church on the Île de la Cité – and distances from the capital to every part of France are measured from the Place du Parvis Notre Dame, the vast square in front of the cathedral.

Notre Dame is known for its sublime architectural balance, although, looking closely, there are minor asymmetrical elements introduced to avoid monotony, in accordance with standard Gothic practice. These include the slightly different shapes of each of the three main portals. Its stained glass windows are a stunning collection of 13th-century Gothic art. Three beautiful rose windows radiate over the west door.

In 1831 Victor Hugo (1802–05) immortalized the cathedral in his novel, *The Hunchback of Notre-Dame*. Descriptions of the cathedral take on such a focal role that many argue they far exceed the requirements of the story, yet they establish Hugo's keen desire to make his contemporaries aware of the value of architecture as a didactic art form, which he feared was in jeopardy with the arrival of the printing press and its ability to bring images to the masses. Happily, Hugo's fears have not been realized and, if anything, the imposing façade and magnificence of 'Our Lady of Paris' do indeed still stand as inspiration for architects today.

The sombre harmony of the gothic façade is a fascinating interplay of horizontal and vertical lines.

# FLUCTUAT NEC MERGITUR
Tossed but not sunk

Emblazoned on the city's coat of arms, this Latin phrase, meaning 'tossed but not sunk', is Paris's official motto. Originally adopted by the river Seine's boatman's corporation, an influential guild that had ruled Paris's trade and commerce since the Roman era, the phrase was officially recognized as the city's motto in 1853 by Baron Georges-Eugène Haussmann (1809–91); see page 24.

Accompanying a picture of a ship sailing on a rough sea, the words and image are believed to represent the strength and resilience that Paris has shown in the face of the hardships she has endured over the course of her history. Its message is simple – no matter how much you rock the boat, Paris will survive – but, above all, the words are a symbol of resistance and a reminder of the strength of Paris's people.

More recently, the motto's meaning has grown in poignancy and significance. In the wake of the terrorist attacks of November 2015 it was used across social media to voice the defiance and determination that Parisians showed in their will to surmount the tragedy. Graffiti of the motto sprung up across the city, most strikingly as a giant fresco in the city's Place de la République, one of its main squares and a traditional site for rallies of protest and demonstration. A café that took the motto as its name now occupies a prominent position on the square.

The coat of arms is made up of crenellated towers, which represent the city, the Seine's boatman's ship referred to in the motto and a fleur-de-lis, the stylized lily that is a potent and enduring symbol of French heraldry. After the 2015 terrorist attacks the city's motto became a symbol of defiance (below).

FLUCTUAT NEC MERGITUR

# THE TUILERIES GARDENS
A place for calm contemplation

The site of former tile factories (*tuileries*), these majestic gardens were created in 1564 by Queen Catherine de Medici (1519–89). They were designed to be admired from the Palais des Tuileries, the residential palace the queen was building for herself alongside them, and were exclusive to the royal court.

A century later André Le Nôtre (1613–1700), who was gardener to Louis XIV (1638–1715), re-landscaped the Italian gardens to impose the order, structure and symmetry of a classic French formal garden style. Le Nôtre's gardens were designed to be seen from above. He eliminated the street that separated the palace from the gardens, replacing it with a terrace that looked down upon parterres. He also opened a central axis along the gardens' length. Le Nôtre's background in mathematics and architecture undoubtedly underpinned his obsession with rigidity and structure, and he wanted this grand perspective to extend outside the gardens, in the form of an avenue that would continue west out of the city. Georges-Eugène Haussmann (1809–91; see page 24) later used Le Nôtre's axis as a basis for his city infrastructure and it become the 'grand axis' of Paris, leading to the Arc de Triomphe (see page 16) and La Défense (see page 66).

After the Revolution of 1789 the Tuileries were opened to the public, and by the 19th century they had become the most fashionable spot in Paris for parading about in one's finery. Today the gardens continue their association with fashion, being a popular choice for shows during Fashion Week.

The gardens are a milestone project in garden architecture and in the development of Paris as an axial city, but, above all, they are an important cultural and historic site within the city, a place of beauty for calm contemplation, enjoyed by Parisians and tourists alike. Home to two art galleries – the Jeu de Paume and the Musée de l'Orangerie – they are also an open-air sculpture museum in their own right, where strollers can wander among 20 bronze statues by Aristide Maillol (1861–1944), Auguste Rodin (1840–1917) and Alberto Giacometti (1901–66).

With two art galleries and sculpture-lined paths, the manicured Tuileries gardens are a draw for their culture as well as their beauty, but above all they're a tranquil, relaxing spot to take a break from the hustle and bustle, set far enough back from the rue de Rivoli to block out the screeching vehicle sounds.

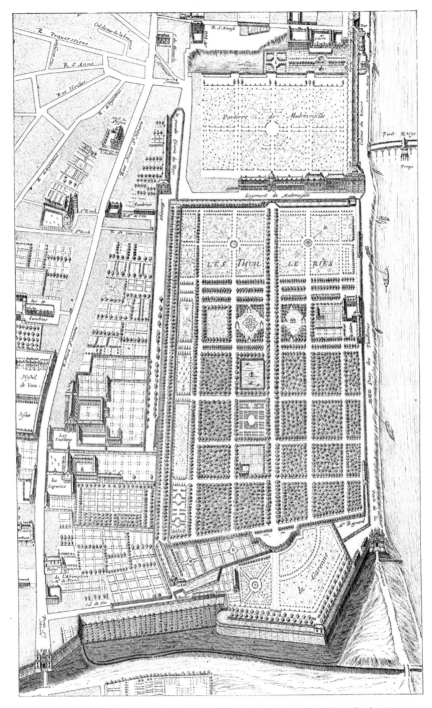

Fig. 22. — Le palais et le jardin des Tuileries en 1632. Fac-simile du plan de I. Gomboust.

# PLACE DE LA CONCORDE
The grandest square in Paris

It is somewhat ironic that the idea for this octagonal-shaped 'square', the execution site of the bloodiest political revolution in France's history, was born from a desire to celebrate a king's recovery from illness. The square itself, still the grandest and largest in Paris, was only secondary to the decision to erect an equestrian statue of Louis XV. After Edmé Bouchardon (1698–1762) was selected to sculpt the statue, it was Ange-Jacques Gabriel (1698–1782) who won a competition to design the square and choose its site, a commanding setting at the head of the Champs-Élysées and adjacent to the banks of the river Seine and the entrance to the Tuileries Gardens (see page 12).

Construction of the square was completed in 1772 but, in 1792 the revolutionaries seized power and tore down the statue of the monarch, replacing it with a guillotine and renaming the square 'Place de la Révolution'. It is hard to imagine the riotous, noisy and terrifying scenes of the executions that took place there when one looks at the serene, sleek Luxor Obelisk that now towers from its central point. The pink granite monolith was given to France in 1829 by the viceroy of Egypt, Muhammed Ali, to thank the country for the groundbreaking work in deciphering hieroglyphs undertaken by the scholar Jean-François Champollion (1790–1832). The ancient monument is decorated with glyphs portraying the reigns of the pharaohs Ramses II and Ramses III, while the plinth on which it stands depicts images of its journey to Paris, which took two and half years – the giant monolith weighs around 230 tons (253 tonne) and stands 23m (75ft) tall. It is flanked on both sides by two magnificent fountains constructed during the same period as the installation and inspired by the fountains on Saint Peter's Square in Rome.

Sadly, no designer could foresee the impact that modern technology would have on this magnificent landmark. Having survived more than 3,000 years, the Obelisk has suffered the greatest damage during the past century from industrial and, more recently, vehicle air pollution, while the beauty of the square itself is all but lost amid a screeching, belching mass of cars trying to cross its cobbles.

The Luxor Obelisk at the centre of the square is one of a pair – the second stands in front of the temple in Luxor. The two fountains flaking either side of the obelisk represent the commerce and industry of France's rivers and the sea.

# ARC DE TRIOMPHE
Symbol of patriotism rising above the Square of the Star

Driving a car in Paris is considered perilous at the best of times, but try to circumnavigate the Place de Charles de Gaulle (more commonly known by Parisians as the Place de l'étoile, its original name) and you take your life in your hands. As the focal point of a star-shaped configuration of 12 radiating avenues (hence its original name, 'Square of the Star'); and with around ten or more tangled lanes of traffic in which nobody strictly has the right of way, the square is as renowned for being an urban hazard as much as it is for its association with the iconic monument it encircles.

Rising out of the centre of the sprawling road junction is the towering Arc de Triomphe, the world's largest triumphal arch (although no longer the tallest), twice the size of the ancient Roman Arch of Titus after which it was modelled. It was designed by architect Jean-François-Thérèse Chalgrin (1739–1811) in 1806 – although work was completed by Louis-Robert Goust (1761–1838) and Jean-Nicolas Huyot (1780–1840) after Chalgrin died – and both its size and design reflect the neoclassical style of architecture popular during the first half of the 19th century. The arch is built on such a large scale that in 1919 French aviator Charles Godefroy famously flew his Nieuport biplane through it to mark the end of hostilities in World War I.

The arch was commissioned by Napoleon I to honour and commemorate the accomplishments of the French armies that had fought in his military conquests, and it remains one of France's most prominent expressions of patriotism. Engraved around the top are the names of major triumphs from the Revolution of 1789 and the Napoleonic Wars (1803–15), as well as the names of less important victories; the names of 558 generals are found on the inside walls. Reliefs by four of France's major academic sculptors – Jean-Pierre Cortot (1787–1843), François Rude (1784–1855), James Pradier (1790–1852) and Philippe Joseph Henri Lemaire (1798–1880) – adorn each of the arch's four pillars, all referencing scenes celebrating French military prowess. Today the arch is still the site of the annual July 14 Bastille Day military parade.

The constantly moving traffic around Place de Charles de Gaulle means that there is no pedestrian access to the Arc de Triomphe from any of its radiating avenues, but it can be reached by pedestrians via an underpass.

# LE BON MARCHÉ
The first modern department store

When Aristide Boucicaut (1810–77) opened Au Bon Marché (its original name) in 1852, he hit upon a groundbreaking commercial model. For the first time, not only were customers offered a range of items and departments under one roof, they were allowed to browse, exchange unwanted items and even order goods by post. Boucicaut wanted to create a unique shopping experience, designed to incite emotion, surprise and, above all, appeal to all the senses.

By 1869 the success of his endeavour allowed Boucicaut to expand and he bought much larger premises, embarking on an expansion project that would go on for almost 20 years. Led by architect Louis-Auguste Boileau (1812–96), then later his son, and constructed under the guidance of engineer Gustave Eiffel (1832–1923), the building was designed to reflect Boucicaut's principal values – marrying unconventionality with elegance. It was a pioneering space with a cast-iron framework featuring stunning Art Deco elements reminiscent of the belle époque. Sadly, many of these elements were destroyed by a fire in 1915.

In keeping with the creative tradition associated with Paris's literary Left Bank, the store opened an art gallery in 1875. It is still the only shop in the world to boast an internal exhibition space, displaying more than 80 works of art and regularly hosting guest artists and exhibitions.

Today the store lacks the glamorous attributes of its former interior, and its purchase by luxury goods conglomerate LVMH is a contested contradiction of the store's original mass-market traditions. Nevertheless, with its vast collection of ready-to-wear designer brands and regular fashion events, it remains a go-to destination for fashion-conscious Parisians and a landmark institution in the city.

The large windows and glass roof of Le Bon Marché were designed to allow as much light as possible to illluminate the goods on display. Andrée Putman (1925–2013), best known for her avant-garde furnishing and interiors, designed the store's sumptuous central escalator for LVMH when it renovated the store in 1990 (below).

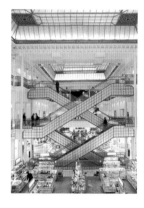

# THE BAGUETTE
The staff of Parisian life

The baguette is an instantly recognizable symbol of Gallic life and has been part of its esteemed culinary history for more than a century – so often copied, yet never rivalled. A true baguette '*tradition*' has a caramel-coloured crust with an unmistakable audible crunch and a creamy crumb with a slightly acidic tang from its natural fermentation. The characteristic shape was born from necessity: in 1919 a law regarding night work was introduced, preventing bakers from starting work before 4am. In order to have enough bread baked for customers waiting in line as the shop opened, they changed the shape of the dough, opting for a longer, thinner loaf that needed a shorter proving and baking time.

In Paris there are thousands of *boulangeries* – there is quite literally one on every street corner – and their significance to Parisians extends beyond being a place to buy bread. *Boulangeries* are a neighbourhood institution, each inviting intense loyalty and rivalry. And, once you have got beyond the choice of *boulangerie*, there is the simple ritual and pleasure in buying one's baguette. It is not considered overly demanding to ask for your baguette how you like it: '*pas trop cuite*' (not too well baked and still soft) or '*bien cuite*' (well cooked). Finally, there is the ritual breaking off of the end of the baguette, the '*croûton*' or '*quignon*', to eat on the way home.

Since 1994, Paris has held the Grand Prix de la Baguette de Tradition Française de la Ville de Paris – an annual competition to find the best baguette in the city, at which more than 200 entries are judged according to five criteria: appearance, bake, crumb, smell and taste. The entrance criteria are strict: each baguette must measure between 55 and 65cm (21½ and 25½in), weigh between 250 and 300g (9 and 10½oz) and contain no more than 18g (¾oz) of salt per kilogram (2lb 3oz) of flour; any baguettes not meeting these requirements are discarded. Competition is fierce and the winner of the prestigious prize has the honour of baking the bread for the president and the Palais de L'Élysée, his official residence, for a year.

Not all baguettes are cut from the same cloth. A 'baguette ordinaire', sometimes called a 'baguette Parisienne' is bright white inside with a crisp crust and is made using yeast. A 'baguette tradition' is the artisanal version – shaped by hand and usually leavened with a *levain*, a sourdough starter.

# THE JULY COLUMN
## Celebrating 'three glorious days' that saw the fall of Charles X

As the site of the eponymous prison until its storming during the Revolution of 1789, the Place de la Bastille has always been a significant Parisian landmark. However, the July Column that stands in its centre raised its impression to new heights.

Originally proposed in 1792 to commemorate the events of 1789, the column was eventually erected in recognition of the *Trois Glorieuses*, the July Revolution of 1830. The victims who died were placed inside a burial vault, out of which now rises the monument, and their names engraved in gold in the cast-bronze drums that make up the column. On top of the column stands the gilded *Génie de la Liberté* (the 'Spirit of Freedom'), crowned with a star and holding a torch that represents civilization in one hand and the broken chains of imprisonment in the other.

The column is a striking and important relic of the 19th century, so it is fitting that the square in which it sits continues to be a lively hub of activity, playing host to a variety of concerts and events as well as political demonstrations. It also stands at the head of what many consider to be 'old Paris'. The square straddles three arrondissements – the 4th, 11th and 12th – and the direction in which one leaves it reflects the history of each. To the east are the few remaining artisan boutiques of the rue du Faubourg Saint-Antoine; north leads to the historic Marais quarter – the oldest in Paris – with its nest of narrow streets and its magnificent Place des Vosges; while the south takes you to the river Seine and the birthplace of the city.

The three glorious days celebrated by the column are 27–29 July 1830, when Louis Philippe I claimed the French throne after the abdication of his cousin, Charles X.

# BARON GEORGES-EUGÈNE HAUSSMANN

The man who created Paris

A divisive figure in the city's history, Georges-Eugène Haussmann (1809–91) was, many would claim, an astounding urban visionary and is the architect of the city we know today. Much of the design and aesthetic of modern-day Paris *is* Haussmann's Paris.

Born in Paris, in a house he later demolished as part of his renovation project, Haussmann rose quickly through the ranks of public administration to be appointed as Emperor Louis-Napoléon Bonaparte's Prefect of the Seine. Haussmann was charged with executing Bonaparte's biggest development project, the 'modernization' and sanitization of Paris.

The streets of Paris in 1853 were dark, dirty, narrow and insalubrious. Haussmann's primary objectives were to increase air circulation and facilitate the movement of people and traffic. His first step was to overhaul the city's infrastructure, opening up axes running from north to south and east to west across the city. Working outwards from the city centre, he evicted the occupants from hundreds of buildings, demolished them, and carved up the city with his wide boulevards. To accommodate the city's growing population, he issued a decree that annexed 11 of its surrounding communes, increasing the number of arrondissements from 12 to 20 and creating the city's modern boundaries.

The Haussmann aesthetic was rational and uniform: avenues were laid in straight lines and the buildings along them were subject to strict architectural guidelines – regardless of function or purpose, they were required to be the same height, fronted with the cream-coloured stone he favoured. Although some landmarks were sacrificed in order to achieve his aims, many besides were created. It is also thanks to Haussmann that Paris continues to enjoy the greenery and relaxing spaces of the Bois de Vincennes, the Parc Montsouris, the Parc des Buttes-Chaumont and the many garden squares that pepper the city's neighbourhoods.

Haussmann's critics have accused him of squandering public money, engendering social division and exclusion, and of poor planning, as well as questioning his motives, yet his legacy remains undeniable. Buildings designed in the Haussmann style are still hotly in demand among residents purchasing or renting property in the city, with prices reflecting their appeal accordingly.

Although Louis XIV had begun the construction of a ring of wide boulevards in the city during his reign, it was Haussmann who further developed the 'boulevard', opening up a large network of interconnecting wide avenues. Today the boulevard named after the man himself is the site for two of Paris's most famous shops – Galeries Lafayette and Printemps.

# PALAIS GARNIER
A place to see and be seen

The Paris opera house, named after its architect, Charles Garnier (1825–98), is considered one of the most prominent architectural masterpieces of its time. The most expensive building erected under Haussmann's reconstructions (see page 24), it remains one of exceptional opulence and a grand tribute to the performing arts.

Garnier described his work as 'the architecture of illustration', and indeed his work can be read like a book. On the outside, our eyes move upwards from the solid ground floor, over its repeated arches sheltering the entrance doors, to the main floor with its wide, paired columns, its balconies and row of round bull's-eye windows, each containing the bronze bust of a composer.

Garnier's style, although many would describe it as particularly flamboyant, is considered representative of the grandiose beaux-arts style prevalent during the Second Empire (1852–70), drawing heavily on axial symmetry and an abundance of Neo-Baroque decorative elements, which all combine to reflect not only the building's purpose, but also the social norms of the time. The Paris opera house was also designed as a social gathering space – a place to see but also to be seen – and its interweaving corridors, stairwells, balconies and alcoves allowed for movement of large crowds but also enabled those in them to gaze outwards or seek the regard of others.

The scale of the architecture is unrivalled: the auditorium can seat more than 2,000 people, while the stage – the largest ever constructed – was built to accommodate up to 450 artists. It is magnificently decorated with marble friezes, columns and statues, many of which portray deities from Greek mythology.

After the classicism of Garnier's rich neo-Baroque effects, however, the eye finally arrives at the auditorium's apex, only to be met with discord: a mid-20th-century ceiling. Painted on canvas by Marc Chagall (1887–1985), the controversial ceiling was installed on a removable frame over the top of the original work by Jules Eugène Lenepveu (1819–98). When it was unveiled in 1964, Chagall's patchwork of operatic scenes, painted in a torrent of 'surrealistic' colours, attracted criticism and outrage; for many it continues to mar the perfection of Garnier's original design.

The grand foyer, at 54m (59yd) long, is one of the most dazzling rooms inside the opera house. Decorated with chandeliers, gold and an exquisite ceiling depicting the history of music painted by Paul Baudry, it was originally intended as a place to take a break, mingle and, in some cases, conduct business. It is purposely located just outside the most expensive boxes.

# MONTMARTRE STAIRS
## Climb to a panoramic outlook over Paris

Montmartre is often talked about by Parisians the way New Yorkers talk about their Village: as a commercialized 'Disneyland', a playground for film-makers and a honeypot for tourists, from which generations of longstanding locals and, in this case, artists, have been evicted because its charming cobbled streets have become so desirable that they can't afford to live there anymore. There is a degree of truth in this, yet there is much still to love about this singular and special neighbourhood, perched on a hilltop and steeped in the romance for which the city is so famous.

You may have to jostle for space, but climbing the 222 stairs that run alongside the neighbourhood's funicular is undoubtedly one of the most breathtaking (and energetic) ways to see the city. Famously captured by Brassaï (1899–1984) in the early morning mist, the peculiarity of the steep stairs is that they make up the rue Foyatier, yet they are the only element to the 'road'; nobody lives there and the only building to take the street's name as an address is a primary school.

Reaching the top, and therefore the foot of the gleaming white Sacré-Cœur Basilica, rewards the intrepid climber with one of the most remarkable, panoramic views of the city, taking in many of its most iconic landmarks.

Sitting at the summit of the *butte Monmartre*, the Sacré-Cœur Basilica is remarkable not only for its prominent position, but also for its brilliant colour. It is constructed from Château-Landon stone, which is known for its high content of calcite. In damp weather calcite leaches out of the stone, keeping the appearance of the monument chalky white.

# THE TROCADÉRO
The best view of the Eiffel Tower

Paris is a city of noble public places and Parisians have a deep commitment to the sense that their city is a public space for them, to be enjoyed and celebrated. The site known as the 'Trocadéro', which refers to the Palais de Chaillot, as well as its expansive esplanade and manicured gardens, is a prime example of this. Housing three museums, a theatre and an aquarium, the Palace attracts a steady stream of tourists and arts lovers. The esplanade and gardens are best known, and not to be missed, for the stunning view they afford of the Eiffel Tower (see page 34), and their sense of grandeur. A direct counterpoint to the tapered tower, which sits on the southern side of the river Seine, the sprawling gardens provide the perfect viewpoint for the New Year's Eve fireworks display, and are a beautiful, if lively, place to while away a few hours, listening to the gentle splash of the fountains and water arches. They are a rare example of a grand open space in a city often known for its narrowness.

The first structure built on top of the hill was erected for the 1878 Exposition Universelle. Architecturally it was an unusual building, showcasing elements of Moorish as well as Byzantine design. In 1937, when Paris again hosted the Exhibition, it was demolished and rebuilt as the Palais de Chaillot. The architects, Louis-Hippolyte Boileau (1878–1948), Jacques Carlu (1890–1976) and Léon Azéma (1888–1978), opted for a very modern architectural vocabulary, representative of the 1930s: a gleaming white façade interposed with pilasters and cornices.

It is in the Palais de Chaillot that the United Nations General Assembly signed the Universal Declaration of Human Rights on 10 December 1948. The event is commemorated with a stone, and the esplanade is now known as the '*esplanade des droits de l'homme*' ('esplanade of human rights').

The centrepiece of the Trocadéro gardens is the Fountain of Warsaw, a long water mirror with 12 fountains jetting 12-m (39-ft) columns of water, ten water arches and 24 smaller fountains.

# CAFÉ DE FLORE

A literary institution where the fashionable gather

One of the most emblematic and evocative symbols of Paris life, the Parisian bistro is a place to drink coffee, sip a glass of wine and snack on a plate of cheese, or to order simple, traditional dishes from a menu that seldom changes. Visitors flock to Paris hoping to chance upon the perfect, cosy corner specimen, the ideal spot to watch the world go by. While the Café de Flore delivers all this in spades, it has also managed to preserve its reputation as a meeting place for the intellectual elite and the cream of fashionable Parisian society, without succumbing to the touristic clichés of its neighbours.

It was during the 1920s that the Left Bank forged its reputation as the literary hub of the city and its cafés became the meeting point for writers, philosophers and intellectuals and, later, actors and artists. Editors held court at bistros along the Boulevard Saint-Germain, looking for manuscripts, and writers were free to work for hours at a café table, fortified by the occasional *eau de vie* or Alsatian beer. By its heyday in the 1930s, the Café de Flore seemed to boast more literary clientele than chairs. The café's classic Art Deco interior of red banquette seating, mahogany furnishings and wide mirrors has changed little since then, and editors from the neighbourhood's publishing houses still hold hushed meetings there, eschewing the bustling and popular terrace for the quieter upstairs, deemed the height of chic.

The awards ceremony for the Prix de Flore, a literary prize founded in 1994 rewarding promising young authors, is held at the café annually. Its winner is presented with a large sum, as well as the opportunity to enjoy a glass of Pouilly-Fumé there every day for a year. The Café de Flore remains the face of the intellectual life of the neighbourhood and a Paris institution.

Parisian literary history has always portrayed the café as a hub that drew writers like mosquitoes to light. Guillaume Apollinaire (1880–1918), Jean-Paul Sartre (1905–80), Simone de Beauvoir (1908–86) and Ernest Hemingway (1899–1961) are just some of the legendary clientele that chose to frequent the Café de Flore.

# THE EIFFEL TOWER
The most famous sight in all of Paris

The Eiffel Tower is *the* symbol of Paris, a feat of architectural engineering, a visual signpost, a glittering beacon in the skies of the capital and the most visited paid-for monument in the world.

Organizers of the 1889 Exposition Universelle, which commemorated the 100-year anniversary of the fall of the Bastille and the start of the French Revolution, staged an open competition for the opportunity to design a spectacular centrepiece to the fair. The vision of the selected engineer and designer, Gustave Eiffel (1832–1923), was to astonish crowds with the tallest building in France. He succeeded. The Eiffel Tower was nearly double the height of the world's previous tallest structure – the Washington Monument – a feat that would not be surpassed until the completion of New York's Chrysler Building 41 years later. Originally intended to stand for 20 years, the tower was almost torn down in 1909; it was saved by Eiffel's decision to erect an antenna on the top and finance experiments in sending and receiving wireless messages. These were particularly valuable for the military and the government abandoned the demolition.

Eiffel was selected on the basis of his unrivalled accomplishments in metalwork; the design was conceptualized using the principles of bridge structures, which his engineering company had mastered. Constructed from puddled iron, the tower consists of four columns of latticework girders separated at the base and meeting at the top of the structure with metal girders at regular intervals. One of the key features is its system of elevators. The glass-cage machines selected by Eiffel were made by Otis Elevator Company in the United States as no French company was able to meet the required technical specifications. The technical achievements marked a defining moment of the industrial era. There are 1,665 steps so most people take the lifts, which travel a combined distance of 103,000km (64,000 miles) a year, two and a half times the circumference of the earth.

Like all towers, it allows us to see and be seen but has a unique panoramic view of Paris. Every evening, the Eiffel Tower is lit up until 1am and 20,000 light bulbs bring the monument to life as it sparkles for 5 minutes every hour on the hour.

Considering the rudimentary means available at that time, the Eiffel Tower was erected at record speed. A team of 300 workers took only five months to build the foundations and 21 to finish assembling the metalwork. Following the 2015 Paris attacks, illustrator Jean Jullien (b. 1983) chose to express his sadness by creating an illustration of the famous icon as a symbol of peace.

# HERMÈS
The quintessence of haute couture luxury

It is the story of legend: the journey from a small workshop in Paris, making fine horse saddles and equestrian accessories, to the creation of the most exclusive handbag in the world. A family-owned label for five generations, Hermès is the epitome of French haute couture and luxury. Yet unlike other high-fashion houses, it is much more than just a fashion brand – owning an Hermès product has become a kind of style currency. Hermès sets trends while also managing to immortalize its products.

Despite economic downturn, the demands of the industry and the tightening competition, the company has continued to grow – expanding its range and even diversifying into other areas such as homewares. Most admirably, the brand has stayed true to its founding principles and rich history and has continued to emphasize the value of hand-craftsmanship, making its survival within the challenges of modern markets all the more remarkable.

Since 1950, when actor Grace Kelly (1929–1982) was first seen carrying the '*Sac à dépêches*' and the bag was renamed the Kelly, the pieces have become icons in themselves. The '*carrés*' – the 90 x 90cm (35½ x 35½in) square silk scarves – are a hallmark of pedigree and chic (one is allegedly sold every 20 seconds) and the Birkin bag has the longest waiting list – six years – for any accessory.

In 1837 Thierry Hermès (1801–78) opened his leather workshop in the Grands Boulevards. When his son Charles-Émile Hermès took over the business in1880, he decided to move the workshop to a different address near the president's residence, which had recently been transferred to the Palais de L'Élysée. Hermès chose 24 rue du Faubourg Saint-Honoré, which remains the company's headquarters and flagship boutique to this day.

# PARIS MÉTRO ENTRANCES
Hector Guimard's Art Nouveau legacy

The architect Hector Guimard (1867–1942) is widely considered to be the most prominent representative of the French Art Nouveau style of decoration and architecture, yet his career was, in fact, fleeting; Guimard's best and most prolific period of creativity lasted little more than 15 years, and his greatest success is undeniably the entrances to the Paris Metro.

Commissioned to mark the station entrances and, above all, to enhance the new method of transport and make it more appealing to Parisians, Guimard's designs are quintessential examples of Art Nouveau style and remain among the most admired. His stylized, giant vines drooping under the weight of what appear to be tropical flowers, actually amber glass lamps that light the entrances, draw on the movement's driving inspiration, nature.

Parisians were initially unsure what to think of Guimard's gates. The Art Nouveau movement had been limited to a wealthy clientele in the art world, but the gates soon grew in popularity and eventually become a valued and praised addition to the city landscape. Although they have been faithfully restored and reproduced in cities and museums outside of Paris – New York's Museum of Modern Art purchased one to plant in their garden – only a handful remain in the city today.

Guimard designed two types of entrance – with and without glass roofs. The roofed entrances, known as *édicules* (kiosks), feature a fan-shaped glass canopy; only two examples of this style remain: at Porte Dauphine, as pictured, and Abbesses. Later designs (below) for signposts marking the metro entrances are less lavish but remain decorative and attractive.

# PLAN DE PARIS PAR ARRONDISSEMENT
An exquisitely detailed guide to the streets of Paris

Paris is defined by its arrondissements, not only geographically, but also culturally, aesthetically and psychologically. For Parisians, the districts that make up the inner city – which are only ever referred to by number – and the choice of which you opt to make your home are loaded with supposition. There are almost tribal behaviours and sartorial codes that characterize each neighbourhood.

So this little pocket book, which divides the city into its 20 arrondissements, each with a double-page, easy-to-read map, was once an indispensable resource for anybody navigating its streets. Sadly, it is now almost a relic. Developments in technology mean that the guide has been replaced by the trendier, faster and, many would argue, more practical maps and 'mapper' apps that smartphones and the internet provide.

Many publishing houses do still publish an edition but the most striking and memorable is the original Leconte edition, with its modest typographic cover design and its elegant 1930s typeface. Digital converts would argue that a physical book – a fossil – cannot compete with the interactive immediacy of the digital world. Yet, surely, it is interaction with one's surroundings that is lost through a device which does your thinking for you. In a sense, the layout and structure of the book, as well as its index of street names and major buildings, enable the user to get up close and personal with the city. The user has to relate to, and work with, the material in a way that allows them to truly engage with their surroundings, their sense of direction and the physical distances involved in undertaking a journey.

It is not clear which year the *Plan* was first published, but it was some time after 1920. Until 1928 the little maroon guides were published by L Guilmin, as shown at the bottom of the front cover on early editions. Between 1928 and 1931, they were published by L Guilmin and A Leconte jointly, and from 1942 onwards we find them embossed with A Leconte, as per the book pictured here. The Leconte editions are also likely to be covered in embossed paper, rather than the cloth found on the Guilmin versions.

# THE LOUXOR
Egyptian-inspired home of 'the seventh art'

Despite the pull of television and other more immediate forms of screen entertainment, Parisians' devotion to 'the seventh art' – as Italian film theoretician Ricciotto Canudo (1877–1923) dubbed cinema – prevails. Arrive at a cinema on a weekend without having reserved your seat and you will most likely be turned away. So it was to much fanfare and delight that the stunning Louxor cinema re-opened its doors in 2013, after lying mummified for 30 years.

If the birth of the moving picture dates from Louis Lumière's first paid film projection in 1895, the Louxor grew up alongside the development of the 'movie'. The businessman Henri Silberberg bought the Haussmann-style building in 1919 to profit from the burgeoning industry. Although Egyptology was becoming fashionable in 1920s Paris after the discovery of Tutankhamun's tomb in 1922, the Louxor is the only example of a building drawing inspiration from Ancient Egypt. Its Art Deco façade, composed of cobalt blue, black and gold mosaic tiles, relies on traditional motifs, such as the beetle and cobra; even the building takes its name from the town built on the ruins of the ancient city of Thebes.

After its opening in 1921, the majestic cinema enjoyed six decades of vibrancy and, despite dwindling attendance during the Second World War, is one of the only pre-war cinemas to survive. In 1981 the significance of the building to the city was recognized and the roof and façade were awarded historic-monument status.

Renovated to replicate the original 1920s design, the cinema now boasts two additional screening rooms. What was left of the décor from the original screening room has been carefully preserved behind the new walls, which were fashioned to replicate the originals exactly.

Today the Louxor is something of a contradiction. At the heart of the animated Barbès neighbourhood, the colourful building still sits awkwardly between its 19th-century Haussmann neighbours. Barbès has for some time been an area known for its social friction, yet the cinema has brought new life and a new focal point to the *quartier*. On the one hand its a sign of the gentrification that continues to smother the city, but also an uplifting reminder that France's 'seventh art' transcends social division.

In 1929 the Pathé cinema became manager then owner of the Louxor. The Louxor-Palais du Cinema became the 'Louxor-Pathé', a name that was hard to miss due to its brightly lit sign.

# MAISON LA ROCHE
Striking 1920s architecture

Le Corbusier (1887–1965) was one of the pioneers of modern architecture, so it is no surprise that his third commission in Paris is a striking and singular piece of architecture. Also known as the La Roche-Jeanneret House, it is, in fact, a pair of semi-detached houses, built by Le Corbusier and Pierre Jeanneret (1896–1967), his cousin and long-term design partner, between 1923 and 1925. Raoul La Roche, a Swiss banker and art collector, commissioned the pair to construct a dual-function villa – a gallery for his art collection but also a domestic living space.

The buildings are laid out at right angles to each other and reflect the architectural style and ideas that Le Corbusier was developing during the 1920s. They are constructed from the reinforced concrete he had mastered and adopted from his former employer and mentor Auguste Perret (1874–1954). The blank, white, geometric forms setting off the curved two-storey gallery space were the fruits of a new, modern architectural language, representative of Le Corbusier's overriding aim, which was practicality over aesthetic.

Maison La Roche is now a museum – which describes itself as the world's largest collection of Le Corbusier drawings, studies and plans – and a UNESCO World Heritage Site. For the design scout, its situation is also notable: wander through Paris's 16th arrondissement to seek it out and you will stumble upon a pocket of significant French architectural work. Maison La Roche is just around the corner from the rue Mallet-Stevens, named after one of France's greatest inter-war architects, Robert Mallet-Stevens (1886–1945) and the location for five of his houses, as well a number of Perret's Parisian masterpieces.

The architects clearly delineated the two separate roles for the building: the residential space is situated in one half and the gallery is in the other. The pilotis raised the domestic space, enabling the architects to reclaim the area beneath it and create a garden.

# MAISON DE VERRE
A sparkling architectural gem

The ethereal quality of glass allows for some extraordinary architectural creations, but none has gained as much of a reputation for exclusivity or intrigue as the Maison de Verre. The 'House of Glass' was a collaboration between the French furniture and interior designer Pierre Chareau (1883–1950), the Dutch architect Bernard Bijvoet (1889–1979) and the French metal craftsman Louis Dalbet. Built between 1928 and 1932, it represents a milestone in early modern architecture and a fascinating juxtaposition of 'industrial' materials, such as steel beams, with home furnishings.

The building was commissioned by Dr Dalsace and his wife after they bought the site on the Left Bank with the intention of demolishing the existing 18th-century building, and replacing it with a modern home and medical practice. However, the tenant on the top floor refused to sell and the Maison de Verre had to be constructed beneath it, without disturbing the original top floor. Viewed from the courtyard, the house, which is set back from the street, looks like a glowing translucent box. The glass façade is made up of glass blocks, supported by a steel frame structure, and perched on top is the old one-storey apartment.

Since 2006 the house has belonged to Robert M Rubin, a retired American financier, who opens the house to a limited number of tours each month. Anybody fortunate enough to secure one of the coveted places will discover that the interior is perhaps even more impressive than the exterior. Both functional and artistic, it is brought to life by rotating screens and sliding doors in glass, sheet or perforated metal, rolling ladders and retractable staircases, reminding us that the house was designed to be lived in as well as admired.

The glass bricks that make up the walls of the front of the house and part of its rear are flat on one side and domed on the other. During the day, natural light enters the house; at night, industrial spotlights add artificial illumination. A weight-and-pulley system opens the window panels, allowing for natural ventilation. This unique system results in a minimum of visual impact on the structure.

# COCO CHANEL AND HER LOGO
## The essence of chic

Gabrielle Bonheur 'Coco' Chanel (1883–1971) transformed the face of female fashion. She pioneered a change in attitude that freed women from the buttoned-up, restrictive and uncomfortable garments of the 19th century, such as corsets, and for the first time in fashion's history prioritized comfort over aesthetic. Borrowing elements of menswear and emphasizing a casual look, she created elegant, relaxed designs that were truly revolutionary.

Chanel opened her first shop on the rue Cambon in 1910, selling hats. The 1920s saw her label thrive and she began selling clothes and launched her first perfume, Chanel No. 5 – the first to feature a designer's name. In 1925 she launched her now-classic innovation, the Chanel suit, with its collarless jacket and fitted skirt, as well as the 'little black dress', taking a colour once associated with mourning and showing how chic it could be for evening wear.

The Chanel logo is one of the most iconic and recognizable in the fashion industry – a confident, clean symbol of the brand, consisting of two interlocking and opposing letter Cs. It was designed by Coco Chanel herself in 1925 and, unlike many other houses, which have undergone rebrands, it has remained unchanged ever since.

In the capital of haute couture, Chanel – both the woman and the brand – is the essence of chic. Her personal style – simple yet sophisticated outfits, clean lines and neutral colours – is timeless and laid the foundations for the elusive 'Parisienne' style, the effortless elegance that women around the world dream of emulating.

The House of Chanel, now with Karl Lagerfeld at its helm, continues to transcend boundaries. It remains youthful yet classic, popular yet exclusive, and as relevant and attractive to women of a certain age from the western Paris suburbs, dressed in its tweed suits, as it is to young, feisty, fashion-conscious career women in New York.

Pieces such as the iconic tweed suits that Coco Chanel wore herself are timeless classics. Chanel's use of the now legendary fabric was inspired by menswear. After borrowing sportswear from her lover, the Duke of Westminster, Chanel admired the supple quality of the fabric, which embraced the principal of comfort that was at the heart of her design.

# PALAIS DE TOKYO
Pared-back contemporary architecture

Designed in 1937 for the Exposition Internationale, the building referred to as the 'Palais de Tokyo', named after the avenue de Tokyo on which it was built (later renamed the avenue de New York), was designed to house two separate modern art collections: those of Paris and the French state. The streamlined, stone-clad 1930s exterior, which hugs two sides of a grand piazza, still houses the Musée d'Art Moderne de la Ville de Paris, located in the east wing of the building; the western half has a more chequered history.

Billed as many things, the modern art space was eventually sidelined in the 1970s after it was eclipsed by the opening of the Pompidou Centre in 1977 (see page 54). In 1999 the new Culture Minister launched a scheme to consign part of the west wing to the promotion of contemporary art. Anne Lacaton (b. 1955) and Jean-Philippe Vassal (b. 1954) were the architects charged with the conversion work, a choice that has led to one of the most extreme, exciting and unusual contemporary art spaces in the world.

The work required to expand the space from 7,000 to 22,000m² (75,000 to 237,000ft²) meant gutting the building. The architects admired the honesty of the raw, naked interior stripped back to its concrete frame and chose to embrace it as a feature. The peeling paint, protruding nails, period handrails and cavernous space of the industrial-style interior, while undoubtedly posing problems for certain exhibition curators, give the museum a look of being slightly unfinished, yet it is an arresting discovery for a visitor.

Lacaton and Vassal also wanted to retain the building's connection with the outside world and, while the basement has a sombre, ghost-like aura, the upper levels of the museum are bathed in the light that floods in from the enormous skylights.

In 2012 the museum initiated the Lasco Project. Street artists are invited to put their own stamp on the building's subterranean passages, creating one of the most intriguing programmes of urban art in modern times and adding yet another string to the bow of this extraordinary ode to art and design.

The museum's progamme is vibrant, bold, eclectic and pioneering. It is driven by a desire to change our perception of art and is open to all means of artistic expression.

# LE MONDE

The iconic logo of 'a voice for France'

*Le Monde* is France's daily newspaper of record and one of the most widely respected in the world, thanks to its editorial integrity and independence. The newspaper is relatively modern by broadsheet standards; it was founded in December 1944, under the orders of General Charles de Gaulle, to replace the outdated and now defunct *Le Temps*. Yet in its short history *Le Monde* has quickly become a model of quality, instantly recognizable and prominent on newsstands, thanks to the bold gothic-style lettering of its iconic logo which it adapted from the original 19th-century version on *Le Temps*. De Gaulle wanted a serious, respected voice for France, a newspaper of 'quality' and the logo, which has remained largely unchanged since the paper's creation, is integral in cementing this impression.

In 1994 the typographer Jean François Porchez (b. 1964) approached the paper, offering to modernize and streamline the historic logo, respecting its original design but polishing the shapes and details to make the typeface more readable and better adapted to French culture and modern reading media. The x-height was enlarged to improve the impact and contrast on the front page. At the same time Porchez created a custom font for the body text. In 2005, when many European newspapers were trying to revive dwindling physical sales, *Le Monde* overhauled its look again and decided to adopt the Fenway typeface for the body text, but throughout that time *Le Monde* had been the only French newspaper to use custom fonts.

*Le Monde* has been printed in Paris since its inception and it is perhaps most idiosyncratic for its timing. Both Parisians and the rest of mainland France have to wait to enjoy their moment of calm with their *café* and their newspaper. *Le Monde* is not released on to newsstands until midday and its masthead carries the date for the following day, so that subscribers receive it with the correct date at the top.

Workers strike in front of the newspaper's building in November 1984 as *Le Monde* goes through a financial crisis.

# POMPIDOU CENTRE
A radical, 'inside-out' design phenomenon

Astonishment was the overwhelming reaction to the announcement in 1971 that the then unknown British architect Richard Rogers (b. 1933) and his Italian partner Renzo Piano (b. 1937) had been chosen as the winners of President Georges Pompidou's international competition to find an architect for his cultural centre. And perhaps most surprised of all were the architects themselves.

Now one of the world's most famous and, above all, radical buildings, the Pompidou Centre put Rogers and Piano on the map. They were asked to turn the site of a rundown car park, vacant since the 1930s, into an art institution to champion modern art, but also to create a space that was unlike any traditional museum or art gallery, which Pompidou believed were often alienating to the general public.

Drawing inspiration from the work of the British architect Cedric Price (1934–2003), known for his experimentation with open forms and flexible spaces, Rogers and Piano designed the building to maximize its internal space, creating an exoskeleton that placed the building's infrastructure and mechanical systems on the outside. The result is a motley of bright colour-coded tubes, each colour denoting its function: blue for ventilation, green for plumbing and fire prevention, yellow and orange for electrical elements, and red for elements that allow for movement throughout the building. One example of the structure's most striking of these 'movement' elements is the escalator tube (painted red underneath) that snakes up to the top of the building. It affords those inside it an extraordinary panoramic view of the city while, from the street, onlookers are treated to a striking animation as the small figures squeezed inside move around the often crowded transparent tube.

Welcoming more than 25,000 visitors daily, it is safe to say that Pompidou's aim – that the centre would be a monumental attraction – has been realized.

The constructivist style of the design of the Pompidou Centre and the use of highly technical custom-fabricated elements to create the structure were unlike anything previously undertaken in the architectural world.

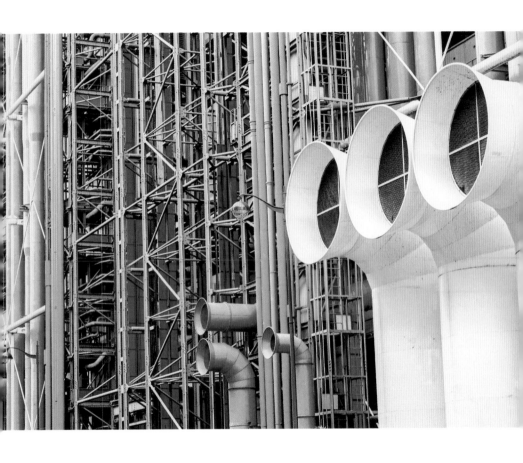

# LE PONT NEUF
## Paris's most seductively beautiful bridge

Despite its name (meaning 'new bridge'), Le Pont Neuf is the oldest bridge in Paris and has joined the Left and Right banks and the Île de la Cité, the birthplace and heart of Paris, for more than 400 years. Flanked by the 14th-century façades of the Left Bank quays and the former La Samaritaine department store on the Right, it crosses the island to set off the Square Vert-Galant, the garden at the island's western tip, which is dominated by an equestrian statue of Henri IV.

The bridge's construction, spanning the reigns of two kings, has a momentous history. Its first stone was laid in 1578; the last was put into place 30 years later after construction had to be paused during the Wars of Religion. The bridge was given its name by Henri IV to distinguish it from its older neighbours, which were all lined with houses. It was his decision to keep the bridge for pedestrians, carriages and horses, so as not to impede the clear view on to the Louvre.

The bridge has long inspired artists working in a variety of cultural domains: the first attempt at daguerreotype by Louis-Jacques-Mandé Daguerre (1787–1851) is believed to have been taken of the equestrian statue; Leos Carax (b. 1960) set and shot his troubled film *Les Amants du Pont Neuf* (1991) in and around its archways; and in 1985 the art duo Christo and Jeanne-Claude (b. 1935 and 1935–2009), known for their ambitious feats, draped the venerable Parisian landmark in more than 41,000m² (441,000ft²) of fabric trussed with rope to create their temporary artwork, *The Pont Neuf Wrapped*.

The bridge is composed of 12 arches, divided between two spans – seven connect the Right Bank to the Île de la Cité and another five join it to the Left Bank.

# MUSÉE PICASSO
Showcasing one of Paris's most beloved art collections

The personal collection of pieces that was discovered when Pablo Picasso (1881–1973) died, believed to amount to more than 70,000 items, was dumfounding. Even his most intimate friends and family were unaware of the scale of his output. It took almost a decade to organize his legacy but in 1985, the beloved Musée Picasso opened in Paris. As well as the state archive of some 200,000 pieces, the Picasso family had donated more than 5,000 artworks to the French state under a law permitting heirs to contribute art in lieu of inheritance tax. Public curators were given first choice of the inheritance, enabling them to pick the very best of the undiscovered treasures.

The museum has always enjoyed a dual appeal: the scale of its astonishing collection, but also the *hôtel particulier* in which it is housed, a regal 17th-century townhouse in the historic Marais district. Built in the 1650s for Pierre Aubert de Fontenay, collector of the *gabelle* (salt tax), which gave it its name, the 'Hôtel Salé', the building was a natural choice for an artist whose work had been created in private mansions and other historic buildings, but it was also a striking and deliberate architectural contrast to the Pompidou Centre (see page 54) nearby.

The choice posed a challenge for the architect Roland Simounet (1927–1996): how to appropriate a residential home for an exhibition space, while respecting the listed elements of the building, its superb stucco and stone décor. The modernist white boxes he designed succeeded in lending the interior an intimate feeling.

In 2009 the museum closed for what became a refurbishment project steeped in controversy. Five years later, after several missed opening dates, Laurent Le Bon, former head of the Pompidou Centre in Metz, replaced Picasso scholar Anne Baldassari to preside over the opening. Family members criticized the museum's disorganization but the space has doubled in size, many more works are on display than ever before, and the queues speak for themselves.

The Hôtel Salé is one of the most extravagant and lavish townhouses found in the Marais. The central staircase is its masterpiece, based on the stair plan designed by Michelangelo in 1524 for the Laurentian Library in Florence. The stairs are overlooked by a protruding balcony and a gallery and display a permanent collection of Picasso works, including *Bust of a Woman (Marie-Thérèse)*, 1931.

# BUREN'S COLUMNS
Candy-striped controversy

French conceptual artist Daniel Buren (b. 1938) created the stark installation *Les Deux Plateaux* ('The Two Levels') in 1985–6. What is so visually appealing and interesting to many – and a complete abomination to others – is its bold, confident confrontation with its surroundings.

Poking out of the courtyard of the 17th-century Palais Royal, Buren's 260 black-and-white candy-striped marble columns, set at different heights, were, and to a lesser degree still are, fiercely controversial, deemed to be a wholly inappropriate and baffling juxtaposition of modern and ancient. And yet supporters would argue that this was, in fact, the whole point. The installation was commissioned as one of President François Mitterrand's *Grands Projets* – a programme to represent the advance of a more open-minded, dynamic France in which modern creations would equal, even rival, the great artistic achievements of the past.

Modern structures have always had to fight to exist in Paris. Buren's columns attracted particularly vitriolic criticism from right-wing commentators who felt that they represented both a rejection of, and intrusion into, France's illustrious architectural traditions and the demise of its cultural heritage.

Yet 30 years on, the columns have garnered huge popularity: skateboarders slalom among them, children use them as climbing frames and tourists love to pose in front of them for photographs. Instead of the severity and silence often associated with modern art, one finds a space that has been brought to life through it. The pillars have become props for play, interaction and fun. Even the 'stripes' themselves are a cheerful nod to the stripes that adorn numerous awnings in Paris – an intentional 'loan' of one of the city's prominent visual motifs.

Buren's sculpture marked the first time that contemporary art had been allowed to mingle so freely with the city's esteemed historic architecture.

# MUSÉE D'ORSAY
Unforgettable art in a beautiful location

Railways and their stations never fail to evoke romance and fascination so cynics might say that the idea of housing a museum inside France's greatest 19th-century railway station was a stroke of clever marketing. There is no doubting the romantic appeal of the Musée d'Orsay's architectural beauty.

The stunning beaux-arts Gare d'Orsay had been the terminus for the country's southwestern railway, built to welcome the expected influx of visitors for the Exposition Universelle of 1900. However, in 1939 the platforms were deemed too short for longer, modern trains and the station became defunct. It was successively used as a postal centre, a film set, an auctioneering house and a theatre, until being threatened with destruction. Finally, it was rescued and listed as a Historic Monument in 1978, then designated the site of a museum to house a collection that would bridge the gap between the Louvre and the Pompidou Centre. The Musée d'Orsay remains devoted to arts from 1848 to 1914.

A young architectal team won the competition to create 20,000m² (215,278ft²) of exhibition space, respecting and reinterpreting the station's original structure. The great hall with its ornate Art Nouveau glass awning, designed by Victor Laloux (1850–1937), became the main artery of the museum. Galleries were carved on both sides of its central nave and two more floors of exhibition space and facilities were created above it.

The Italian interior designer Gae Aulenti (1927–2012) insisted that homogenous white stone walls and both natural and artificial light would create the variations in intensity needed for the different works of art. Subsequent renovations have changed the wall and floor colours to grey and dark wood respectively, however, while a combination of halogen and new-generation diode lights have been used to create what is now thought to be the optimum balance of light for setting off the art.

The Musée d'Orsay is most remarkable for what the building itself has come to represent: it is as much of an exhibit as the exhibits themselves. For many, a visit to the towers from where you can view the Sacré Cœur from behind the working clockfaces holds as much appeal as the astounding collection of Impressionist and post-Impressionist paintings.

Upon entering the museum, visitors are quickly reminded that the building was formerly a train station. The curved glass canopy above the entrance recalls the train-shed roofs that were fashionable during the 19th century and covered many large stations, such as the Gare du Nord and the Gare de Lyon in Paris and London's St Pancras.

# A.P.C.
## Tasteful cool

It was a trip to Barcelona, lost luggage and a futile search for well-fitting jeans and sweaters that prompted Jean Touitou (b. 1951) to launch clothing brand A.P.C., his '*Atelier de Production et de Création*' ('production and creation workshop'), to produce the simple style of garment that had eluded him. And for a brand that claims a cult following and could well be described as a fashion icon, it is ironic that its founder really doesn't like 'fashion'. On the contrary, he claims a love for the effortless simplicity of uniform and the timelessness of clean lines and classic silhouettes. Yet, unlike the clothes he designs, one wouldn't describe Touitou as understated; he is known for his outspokenness and is considered by some as something of a renegade within the industry.

One of the brand's most popular products are its raw denim jeans – in France, A.P.C. jeans dethroned the seemingly untouchable Levi's 501s – and denim enthusiasts continue to exalt the quality of the Japanese selvage denim and the slim, perfect-fitting cut of the jeans.

A.P.C. stands for a particular type of tasteful cool. Its androgynous, uniform-like look is minimal and casual – at times it could even be described as austere. Indeed, when the brand was first launched in the late 1980s, many rejected its rigour and restraint. The design has softened a little since then: in 2012 Touitou approached the Argentinian designer Vanessa Seward (b. 1969) and asked her to create a series of capsule collections for the women's line, and she introduced a few subtle, feminine touches – printed silk dresses and tango-esque shoes started appearing. But it is Touitou's steadfast commitment to his aesthetic that is the brand's strength and success and is what continues to enable it to draw fans from across all ages, sizes and fashion tribes.

Plain, minimal and unassuming, the A.P.C. shop fronts reflect the ethos at the heart of the brand.

# GRANDE ARCHE DE LA DÉFENSE
Purity of form

Paris is a city in which architecture is closely entwined with politics. Kings built to assert their power; the urban planning system devised by Baron Georges-Eugéne Haussmann (1809–91) was, in part, a political act (see page 24); and during France's most recent large-scale architectural project, under President François Mitterrand (1916–96), architecture once again seemed to be the prime material for political ambition and legacy.

The tall thicket of glass and concrete towers you arrive at when you follow Paris's western 'Historical Axis' to its end might come as quite a shock. The sea of skyscrapers, where most of the city's tallest buildings can be found, is something of an anomaly in the low-lying, protected Parisian skyline. But La Défense is the city's business district, a bustling enclave that draws more than 100,000 daily commuters. Punctuating the end of the axis is Mitterrand's modernist Grande Arche, designed to be a mirror to the Arc de Triomphe (see page 16). If the former represents Paris's historic past and commemorates military victories, the Grande Arche, which was completed in 1989 to honour the bicentenary of the Revolution, was designed to look to the city's future, to more humanitarian ideals and a different idea of progress.

The architect who won Mitterrand's competition to design the arch was a little-known Danish professor, Johan Otto von Spreckelsen (1929–87), whose previous projects amounted, he claimed, to no more than three churches and a house. Tragically, he died before the arch's completion.

The Grande Arche is an astounding structure, a distinctive example of purist, minimalist architecture. More than 110m (360ft) long, wide and high, the reflective white marble and concrete hollow cube is said to be large enough to enclose Notre Dame Cathedral (see page 8). The only thing interrupting its perfect form is the lift scaffolding, now closed to the public after an accident, and a fibreglass 'cloud' canopy suspended within the hollow.

Although the area around the Grande Arche isn't the most interesting part of the city to visit, the monument's grandeur and scale are breathtaking and worth making the trip for. The views from the steps leading up to the arch allow you to appreciate the exacting precision with which the landmark monuments are stacked along Haussmann's 'Historical Axis'.

# THE LOUVRE PYRAMID
## A much-loved modern landmark

When architect I M Pei (b. 1917) first designed the giant glass structure in the Louvre's central courtyard in the 1980s, critics argued it was 'sacrilegious' to tamper with such a prized jewel in the French architectural crown – a megalomaniacal folly. Others declared it to be an innovative, successful merging of modernism with classicism.

Shortly after he was elected president in 1981, François Mitterrand embarked on his ambitious '*Projet du Grand Louvre*' to modernize and expand the gallery that was renowned as such an international showcase for the French, without compromising its historical integrity. The controversy surrounding the project began with his choice of a Chinese-American architect and the criticisms mounted from there. The success of its aesthetic can be debated eternally, but what is undeniable is that, on a practical level, major works needed to be undertaken at the art gallery simply in order to manage its 4.5 million annual visitors (a figure that has since risen to hover around 10 million). And, more than 20 years on, both Parisians' and visitors' reactions to a structure that functions as the museum's main entrance speak for themselves – it has become one of the Louvre's leading attractions. It has been used as an art installation in its own right, such as in May 2016, when French street artist and photographer JR, famous for his large-scale black-and-white photography, was permitted to cover the pyramid in photographs of the portion of the palace building that is blocked behind it, causing the pyramid to 'disappear'.

The pyramid's universal form is a mastery of technical prowess, but its choice had nothing to do with professional vanity. Pei felt that a pyramid shape was 'most compatible' with other structures at the Louvre, and, acutely aware of the weight of the building's illustrious history, he wanted the structure itself to recall ancient roots in its reference to the pyramids of Egypt.

The pyramid is now a destination in its own right, the third most visited attraction at the Louvre, after Leonardo da Vinci's *Mona Lisa* (c.1503–19) and the *Venus de Milo* (c.100 BCE).

# STADE DE FRANCE
## Heavier than the Eiffel Tower, longer than the Champs-Élysées

Since the 1920s, France had faced the dilemma of when and how to build a national stadium, so the eventual construction of the Stade de France in 1998 was inevitably a project loaded with great expectation. The stadium came about in part as a knee-jerk reaction: France had just lost its bid to host the 1992 Olympic Games to Barcelona, so President Jacques Chirac was looking to boost the nation's sporting morale by winning the tender for the 1998 FIFA World Cup. One of the conditions of selection was that France build a stadium with a capacity of 80,000 seats.

Four architects – Michel Macary (b. 1936), Aymeric Zublena (b. 1936), Michel Regembal (b. 1946) and Claude Constantini (b. 1948) – made up the team chosen to design a building emphasizing clean lines and taking movement, lightness and the universality of sport as its principle themes.

Rising over Saint-Denis like a spaceship, its signature elliptical opaque-glass roof, suspended 42m (138ft) above the pitch by 18 narrow steel rods, is its main feature. 'Heavier than the Eiffel Tower and longer than the Champs-Élysées', as visitors are told on the stadium tour, it is considered an example of huge technical skill, allowing plenty of light to flood the pitch but also completely covering the spectators. The other key feature of the stadium is its retractable lower stands, which can be slid back to reveal an athletics track.

Not only is the stadium a notable mark of France's standing within international sport, it is also an important example of the role that architecture can play in social integration. For a long time, the Saint-Denis suburb was considered an area in need of social, economic and urban renewal, and the building of the Stade de France has indeed succeeded in contributing to the regeneration of the surrounding area.

Despite weighing more than 13,000 tons the stadium's opaque-glass roof feels as if it is floating above the pitch. It is designed to filter out the harmful rays of the sun while letting through those needed to allow the grass to grow properly.

# COLETTE
## Creating trends

Paris's first concept store, opened by Colette Roussaux and her daughter Sarah Lerfel, is an unrivalled temple of fashion: a luxury boutique that has become renowned for limited-edition products and cutting-edge design.

Colette doesn't just spot trends, it creates them; the store famously champions new faces – Rodarte and Nicholas Kirkwood are just two of the international names to have benefitted from its patronage. Above all, the store embraces exclusivity and eclecticism, and seeks to surprise. It brings together luxury fashion brands with street and surf wear, as well as offering the latest in urban and pop culture, technology and beauty products. Colette was one of the pioneers of collaborations and regularly boasts exclusive products by brands ranging from Asics and Valentino to Evian, most quirkily filling its shop windows with Karl Lagerfeld's Barbie and Ken throughout 2009's Fashion Week.

Everything about the store is carefully considered and curated, from the layout and the window dressing, which are changed each week, right down to the packaging. It is a design destination that is constantly reinventing itself. In a city where tribes of shoppers are a common feature, Colette bridges the gap and appeals to shoppers from across the spectrum, from the well-heeled luxury-seeking fashionistas to Paris's expanding collection of hipsters.

Colette's policy is to be new and constantly surprising. As well as carrying established brands, such as Céline, Gucci, Valentino and Adidas, the store supports up-and-coming designers and labels.

# PARC DE LA VILLETTE
The largest discontinuous building in the world

Whatever else can be argued about François Mitterrand's *Grands Projets*, there is no denying that they are all monumental in their public purpose and scope. With the Parc de la Villette and its accompanying cultural complex, Mitterrand took on his most ambitious project in terms of its physical scale, too; one of the last remaining sizeable sites in Paris, a 55-hectare (136-acre) expanse at the northeast corner of the city, previously occupied by the national wholesale meat market and slaughterhouses. The design for the park was selected from more than 470 international competitors.

The brief called for the imagining of an 'urban park' for the 21st century. The proposal by architect Bernard Tchumi (b. 1944) to reject the notion of the traditional recreational green space – where landscape and nature are the predominant forces behind the design – and conceive of it as a space designed with activity as its primary purpose, fitted the objective perfectly. Tschumi wanted to deconstruct the concept of a park and create 'the largest discontinuous building in the world'.

La Villette is an unprecedented type of park, a place of culture where natural and artificial are forced together into a state of constant discovery. It contains more than 25 buildings, including the vast City of Science and Technology and the City of Music – now with its long-awaited, highly controversial concert hall, Philharmonie de Paris, designed by Jean Nouvel (b. 1945) – on the site, as well as promenades, covered walkways, bridges and landscaped gardens. Interspersed throughout the park are Tschumi's 35 iconic red enamelled steel follies – giant twisting structures that are at once industrial and sculptural – designed to help visitors navigate the space and emphasize movement through the park.

Serving as reference points throughout the park, each of Tschumi's 35 follies is different; some have been converted into cafés, restaurants and information centres for the park. The Géode (below) is an eye-catching, reflective sphere which stands outside the City of Science and Technology and houses a 3-D and IMAX cinema.

# GALERIE KREO
A laboratory for art and design

Galerie Kreo, founded by partners Didier (b. 1954) and Clémence (b. 1967) Krzentowski, is widely recognized as one of today's most important and influential design galleries. The pair have been a leading force on the contemporary art and design scene for decades. Opponents of mass-produced industrial pieces, they describe their Paris space as a laboratory, dedicated to producing limited-edition contemporary works, created exclusively for the gallery. And the roster of luminaries is impressive: Jaime Hayon (b. 1974), Pierre Charpin (b.1962), Ronan (b. 1971) and Erwan (b. 1976) Bouroullec and Konstantin Grcic (b. 1965) are among the names on their books.

Alongside the contemporary artwork, the gallery holds an impressive collection of vintage lighting, stemming from Didier Krzentowski's passion for Italian and French lights from the 1940s to the 1980s.

The Krzentowskis opened their gallery in the unlikely 13th arrondissement, later moving it to an arresting space within the art hub of the 6th that combines a 17th-century *hôtel particulier* and a 19th-century Gustave Eiffel conservatory. They now have a second outpost in London's Mayfair.

The couple nurtures each show from conception. They work closely with their designers, reminding them to meet the needs at the heart of design: functionality and use, while also allowing designers the time and creative freedom to focus on their production. The Bouroullec exhibit of 2016, for example, was four years in the making. 'We try to keep the creative cycle alive because it nourishes us,' Didier is quoted as saying. 'For us, design is not just a bunch of objects.'

# MUSÉE DU QUAI BRANLY
A tribute to the diversity of human culture

Museums or their exhibition choices are often subject to debate and controversy, but no opening has perhaps been so bitterly challenged as that of Jacques Chirac's museum of 'the arts and civilizations of Africa, Asia, Oceania and the Americas', his plan to rehouse the national collection of ethnographic art.

Architect Jean Nouvel (b. 1945) also designed François Mitterrand's acclaimed Institut du Monde Arabe (1987) as well as the Foundation Cartier building (1994). He is best known for technologically refined architecture that distorts the way we perceive the world around us, yet here the premise of the museum required greater subtlety. Nouvel wanted to move away from the cutting-edge technical feats of Western architecture and let the building blend into its surroundings, choosing to hide it behind tall trees and an enormous landscaped garden.

The structure itself consists of four buildings. The main body of the museum, perched on concrete piles and steel columns, has a curved shape that allows parts of the garden to grow underneath it, so it appears to be coming out of the greenery. Nouvel's intention was that, as the garden matured, these columns would be hidden from view. Each façade is different: colourful boxes protrude from one, on another there are rust-coloured blinds. But the most striking element of the structure is its '*mur végetal*' – a vertical garden that carpets one side of the museum's administrative offices. Made up of 15,000 plants of 150 varieties, it is an extraordinary living tapestry that seems to defy gravity.

Inside, the four permanent exhibition spaces, displaying more than 300,000 artefacts are housed within a cavernous hall, 200m (656ft) long. Mezzanine platforms at either end offer sweeping views of the exhibits.

Morally and architecturally the building has divided opinions. Some hail the structure as the greatest thing Chirac has ever championed, while others attack it as perpetuating antiquated, colonial views.

Nouvel's bold style of architecture and use of colour is at odds with the structured, uniform façades of the 19th-century Haussmann buildings that are its riverside neighbours.

# VÉLIB'
Bicycle + freedom

With one rental station roughly every 300m (985ft), Paris's astoundingly popular bike-sharing scheme is an integral part of the city's landscape and a fundamental feature of Parisian life.

Introduced to the city after the mayor of Paris, Bertrand Delanoë, witnessed the success of schemes in Lyon and La Rochelle, the Vélib' (a fusion of the French words for bicycle, 'vélo', and freedom, 'liberté') was launched with an ecological aim. It was designed to help create a more sustainable and greener transport system by offering another option for short trips, yet its value extends far beyond this. The Vélib' scheme has been shown to reduce air pollution, ease congestion and parking problems, and be a healthy means of getting around, all of which make the city a more beautiful place to live.

JCDecaux, the outdoor advertising agency, operates and funds the scheme (in return for the somewhat controversial contract for exclusive advertising rights). The company collaborated with designer Patrick Jouin (b. 1967), most notable in Paris as the designer of Alain Ducasse's high-end restaurants, on the bikes' structure and look.

The scheme was launched in 2007 and the statistics to date speak for its success. In the first year there were more than 10,000 bicycles on the road; a year later this had increased to more than 16,000 with 20 million journeys made during that year. Figures in 2016 estimate that more than 75 bikes are rented each minute and bicycle use in Paris, which the city says accounts for 3 per cent of vehicle traffic, has increased by some 40 per cent since 2007. The Vélib' is unquestionably a milestone in ecological design.

JCDecaux and Patrick Jouin were awarded a prize for the design of the bikes and their stands at the Good Design Awards 2009. The awards, one of the most prestigious and oldest, recognize the most innovative and cutting-edge industrial, product and graphic designs created around the world.

# PASSAGE DES PANORAMAS
A characterful maze of hip eateries and charming shops

To enter Paris's labyrinth of glass-roofed shopping galleries, known as '*les passages couverts*', is to step back in time and enter a different world. The forerunners of modern-day malls, more than 100 of the ornate walkways were built during the 19th century, though fewer than 20 have survived. The passages were a symbol of urban life: they allowed one to take a shortcut, shelter from the rain or the commotion of the streets outside, shop, dine or spend a secluded hour in the arms of a lover. Many of the passages were beautifully decorated with mosaic floors, cast-iron framework, marble pillars and decorative clocks, creating the image of Paris as a luxury modern city.

Each passage has a distinct personality, but one of the oldest and most characterful is the Passage des Panoramas, crammed with vintage postcard shops and philatelist boutiques. More recently, the passage has marked itself out as a cutting-edge destination for fashionable Parisian diners. From the gluten-free Noglu to the Gyoza Bar and the highly acclaimed Passage 53, directed by Shin Sato, the first Japanese chef in France to have obtained two Michelin stars, the passage has quickly become a symbol of the city's fast-changing gastronomic scene.

Caffè Stern, brainchild of the Alajmo brothers, of the three-star Le Calendre in Padua, and of Gianni Frasi, a coffee roaster from Verona, is one of the most visually striking restaurants. The former engraving workshop is a listed building, refashioned as a classic Italian *caffè* by Philippe Starck (b. 1949). There are Starckian touches: a wolf draped in jewels guards the entrance and an Alice-in-Wonderland-esque white rabbit holding a pocket watch stares out at diners from an alcove, but what is most evident isn't the quirky designer's touch but the building's carefully preserved soul and history. Dimly lit rooms reveal Maison Stern's original 1800s woodwork, thick golden tapestry and other curiosities from its past, creating a unique and intriguing gourmet dining experience.

A juxtaposition of the finest of old and new: intricate 19th-century metal and glasswork provide shelter for some of the most innovative culinary endeavours in the capital today.

# SAINT-OUEN FLEA MARKET

## For browsing and bargain-hunting

Once upon a time, flea markets (*'puces'*) were places to go to snag a real bargain and one-of-a-kind gems. Sadly, the opposite can now be said of the famous puces in Paris's northern suburb of Saint-Ouen, which has been a victim of its own success. Claiming to be the largest market in the world, the sprawling maze of alleyways and market stands is divided into 14 separate markets. They boast more than 1,500 vendors, all vying for the attentions of fashionable Parisians who are predominantly there to stock up on the expensive antique furniture.

The open-air Marché Paul Bert, one of the most popular, is largely given over to minimalist mid-century modern furniture and Art Deco decorative items. Quirky yet stylish, in among the Eames-style chairs and Jacobsen designs are old zinc café counters, telephones, traffic lights and jukeboxes. And the newest 'vintage village' is the latest market to draw a crowd. Primarily a Habitat store, it stocks some of the brand's iconic pieces from the 1960s, 1970s and 1980s, as well as housing a vintage clothes outlet and a chic little buvette.

Despite the price tags, the puces are hugely atmospheric to wander. And if scouring the stands proves trying, shoppers can join the crowds in search of the market's latest appeal: its gastronomy. They could do worse than settle in among the gourmet-loving antique dealers and hungry hipsters at the Philippe Starck-designed Ma Cocotte restaurant.

Although the market has earned a reputation for drawing serious furniture and design collectors, there are still plenty of interesting knick-knacks and cheaper items to be found.

# GRAND PALAIS
A stunning blend of stone, iron and glass

The Grand Palais arguably served as one of the buildings that would help cement France's reputation as a leader in the arts. The magnificent structure, currently the largest glass and ironwork construction in the world, after London's Crystal Palace suffered a fire in 1936, is a masterpiece of the beaux-arts style, a beautiful combination of a classical stone façade and Art Nouveau ironwork.

It was built for the 1900 Exposition Universelle – a celebration of the achievements of the 19th century and a propeller to accelerate development into the next. The palace was judged a resounding success, a venerable showcase of France's splendour to the world.

In certain respects the success is surprising as, while it is sleek and bold in its presentation, the building is also a hybrid and something of a mishmash in terms of its architecture, its usage and its materials. Even the design is not the conception of a sole artist: three architects collaborated to create three separate sections, brought together under the leadership of Charles Girault (1851–1932), and the work of some 40 contemporary artists embellishes the façades with intricate statues, friezes and other ornamentation.

The site was always intended to achieve durability and it is, perhaps, its flexibility and fluidity of purpose that has allowed it to do so. Neither a museum nor a simple monument, the palace is a landmark attraction that hosts a vast diversity of events and audiences. The main gallery is now a designated site for displaying contemporary art, but everything from antique car shows to fashion shows from some of Paris's top designers can also be found there.

The enormous barrel-vaulted iron and glass conservatory-style roof is unquestionably the most stunning draw of the Grand Palais.

# MIDNIGHT IN PARIS
Woody Allen's ode to the city

The Seine is a dream backdrop for directors, and many have sought to immortalize the city's charm on celluloid in countless films, winding their cameras through the pretty cobbled streets, past the picturesque shopfronts and magnificent stately architecture. The films of Woody Allen (b. 1935) have famously celebrated the romantic side of his native New York, but with *Midnight in Paris* (2011) he shines that spotlight on the city that has also had a strong hold over him. It is a love affair that dates from the 1960s, when he locked himself inside the George V hotel to work on the screenplay for *What's New Pussycat?* (1965).

Allen spent three months filming in Paris – it was his first movie to be shot entirely on its streets – and what emerges is a tender, if clichéd, ode to the city. This unashamed reverence of beauty has been heavily panned for its overly sentimental and naïve portrayal of the city. On the one hand, critics argue, Allen's Paris isn't a city, it is a stage set that doesn't reflect today's architectural realities; the high-rise buildings and social tensions are markedly absent under his lens. Yet the film has also been lauded for a vision of the city that celebrates one of its heydays – the Paris of the central character Gil Pender's dreams, the movable feast enjoyed in the 1920s by Ernest Hemingway and F Scott Fitzgerald, does aptly embody an era. And through this portrayal, Allen's great love for the city is palpable – the small, narrow street that serves as the platform from which Gil makes his nightly journey into the past has no signs of anything having changed since the 1920s. Allen's view celebrates the timelessness of the city and, in that respect, he honours a principle on which the city is founded and continues to stand.

*Midnight in Paris* opens with a lengthy montage of the city as a picture-perfect setting, highlighting many of its most iconic tourist attractions.

# THE DOCKS: THE CITÉ DE LA MODE ET DU DESIGN
A rejuvenating design destination

How to revive a century-old concrete industrial warehouse and bring creative, urban and cultural life to an area considered a wasteland? This was the task that Paris architects Dominique Jakob (b. 1966) and Brendan MacFarlane (b. 1961) were charged with when they took on the renovation of the vast warehouse on the banks of the Seine. On first appearances, it would appear they went for visual shock: it is hard to miss the angular, lime-green, caterpillar-like structure that stretches along the quays between Gare d'Austerlitz and Bercy. It certainly adds colour to an area dominated by nondescript glass and aluminium office towers.

Inspired by the ebb and flow of the river, the architects transformed the building by 'revealing its concrete skeleton'. They created an external 'skin' – the caterpillar – using a metal and glass framework, and topped the project with a panoramic terrace. It is now an all-encompassing hub for fashion and design, a fusion of the fashion school, the Institut Français de la Mode, restaurants, shops, bars, a vast rooftop nightclub and a programme of screenings and exhibitions in various galleries. The terrace is spectacular, and behind the imposing façade Jakob and MacFarlane have succeeded in creating a design destination, that teems with vibrancy, and rejuvenates a neglected part of the city.

At night the illuminated green glass tube strikes a conspicuous pose along the Seine. 'Les Docks' are now a far cry from their original purpose, when the building was used to store goods next to the Gare d'Austerlitz.

# FONDATION LOUIS VUITTON

Challenging our perceptions of what an art gallery should be

Now well into his eighties, Frank Gehry (b. 1929) continues to propel himself forward, and to innovate and challenge the realms of architectural achievement. With more than €100 million reportedly spent on the Fondation Louis Vuitton, commissioned by Bernard Arnault (b. 1949), the chairman and CEO of the luxury-goods conglomerate LVMH, Gehry has created a monumental work unlike anything produced before.

Arnault first met Gehry in 2001 and spoke of his wish to create an institution that would house LVMH's burgeoning art collection, host temporary exhibits and provide a platform for diverse cultural programmes. He wanted the building to be truly visionary and bold – representative of 21st-century architecture, but also of LVMH's engagement with, and commitment to, the arts.

What alighted in the Jardin d'Acclimatation of the Bois de Boulogne in 2014 was a majestic and arresting avalanche of glass sails – 12 curved shields that twist and turn in the architect's trademark style – piled up around white reinforced concrete blocks, which house the gallery spaces. Constructed on the edge of a water garden created especially for the project, and echoing its nautical theme, the sails and surrounding landscape and continually change with the light.

In contrast to the exterior, the 11 gallery spaces inside are a very simply designed series of voluminous rectangular rooms – serene spaces for contemplating the art. Visitors are invited to climb exterior stairways to reach the roof terraces that jostle among the twisting protrusions of the gallery skylights. Arnault and Gehry wanted the building to be attractive and welcoming to families and children who play in the garden, and the potential for discovery and games certainly seems to fulfil this aim.

In terms of innovation, the project has set a benchmark for the use of advanced digital technologies. More than 3,600 glass and 19,000 concrete panels that make up the façade were simulated using mathematical techniques and moulded using industrial robots. New software was developed specifically for sharing and working with the complex design. Similarly, the structure's credentials are strong: the glass roof allows the building to collect and reuse rain water and improves its geothermal power.

Gehry's characteristic glass sails reflect the water, woods and garden around the building, creating an ever-changing display under different light conditions. They give the building a sense of movement.

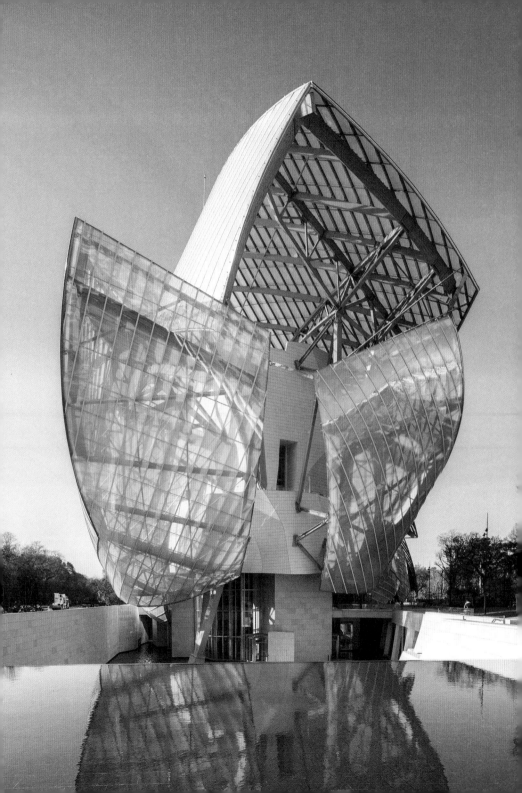

# PLACE DE LA RÉPUBLIQUE
## Reclaiming a French landmark from cars

Marianne – an emblem of freedom and democracy, the symbol and personification of the French Republic – sits atop the centrepiece of the Place de la République, so it is no surprise that this, one of Paris's largest squares, is a significant and rousing landmark for the French. The Ministry of the Interior estimates that after the Charlie Hebdo attacks of January 2015, more than 1.6 million people rallied around the iconic statue to mourn and mark the momentous events – it was the largest public demonstration in modern French history. Tragically, only ten months later, crowds assembled again when Paris was targeted for a second time.

Prior to 2010, the square was essentially a 'glorified roundabout', as mayor Bernard Delanoë described it, when three years later he proudly unveiled its facelift. The convoluted project involved reclaiming ownership of much of the space's 3.4 hectares (8.4 acres) from cars and reallocating more than 70 per cent of it to pedestrians. There is now an all-day café, a children's paddling pool, fountains, sun loungers, armchairs and a vast open space for skateboarders, teenagers playing football or the inevitable demonstrators that continue to flock there.

In 2016 the square became the Parisian site for the spontaneous citizen-led movement '*nuit debout*' ('up all night'). The youth-led cause – which struck up in cities across France and was likened to the 'Occupy' movement of 2011 – triggered striking scenes and the square resembled an overcrowded music festival, with tents, makeshift stalls and activists sitting around cross-legged discussing and denouncing everything from inequality on housing estates to capitalism, exploitation and political alienation.

Although it is a traditional site for protest and demonstration, the square had never experienced a rally as large as that which followed the Charlie Hebdo attacks of 7 January 2015.

# THE BATACLAN
## A beloved site marred by tragedy

The Bataclan takes its name from an operetta by composer Jacques Offenbach (1819–80), but the word is also a pun on the expression '*et tout le bataclan*' ('and all that jazz'). The small concert venue in one of Paris's trendy eastern districts started life in the 19th century, first opening in 1865. It was a classic café-concert hall designed in the Chinoiserie style, like a pagoda, staging mainly vaudeville pieces. Since the 1970s the Bataclan has been a one-of-a-kind legendary venue for rock fans. Its programme is eclectic, although it is most notable in the music arena, with names as diverse as Édith Piaf, Prince, Oasis, Iron Maiden, The Clash and The Police all staging concerts here.

The Bataclan is beloved by an engaged audience of Parisians and rock fans from across the world, yet, heartbreakingly, it has become famous as the site of a tragedy. On 13 November 2015, this humble, joyful entertainment building was the site of one of the greatest terrorist attacks France has ever seen – 90 people were killed and more than 200 wounded when three heavily armed gunmen unleashed their weapons on the crowds on a concert night. The iconic venue is rocking into the future having reopened in November 2016.

Temporarily closed after the 2015 terrorist attacks, the brightly coloured decorative façade remains illustrative of the building's history and welcoming character.

# THE RITZ
Gilded glamour and grace

If walls could talk, the Ritz would undoubtedly have a story or two to tell. Synonymous with luxury, opulence, flawless service, elegance and fine dining, the Ritz has become a symbol of a certain way of Parisian life – a glamorous, aspirational existence oozing with decadence and gilded charm.

In converting the former Hôtel de Gramont on the 18th-century Place Vendôme, Swiss-born César Ritz (1850–1918) had visions of bringing a new level of luxury to Parisian hotels. The hotel should, he said, 'have all the refinement that a prince could desire in his own home'. The Ritz was the city's first hotel with lifts and electricity, and the first in the world to have en-suite bathrooms.

As soon as it opened its doors in 1898, the Ritz became fashionable with the socialites of the day. Coco Chanel (1883–1971) lived there for more than 30 years, and Marcel Proust (1871–1922), Ernest Hemingway (1899–1961) and F Scott Fitzgerald (1896–1940) are among the literary names to have graced its corridors.

In 2012 the Ritz closed its doors for the first time in its history to undergo four years of extensive refurbishment. Thierry Despont (b. 1948), the French-born, New York-based interior designer, was the man charged with steering the project. He wanted to create 'more light and flourish' in the hotel. His plan was to raise the ceiling height in the entrance and open up the windows on the mezzanine, to allow light in. But, although there are modern touches in the hotel's newly glazed courtyard and retractable glass roofs that cover the two restaurants and keep the courtyard terraces open year round, Despont wanted, above all, to stay true to the 18th-century aesthetic, décor and style for which the hotel is renowned. The building's façade is the original, sketched in 1705 by Jules Hardouin-Mansart (1646–1708), chief architect to Louis XIV, and the rooms are fashioned to reflect the hotel's history. The Louis XV armchairs in the dining room still have their handbag hooks under each armrest, as invented by Ritz himself.

Although the renovation project has, of course, attracted criticism, the Ritz remains possibly the most prestigious and luxurious hotel in the world, and certainly the finest and most expensive in Paris.

Much of the décor in today's restored hotel (below) retains the essence of the 19th-century features enjoyed by the glitterati of the day. Televisions are disguised as antique mirrors; gilded turnkeys masquerade as dimmer switches and 19th-century style bell cords still hang next to the marble bathtubs.

# PISCINE MOLITOR
Renaissance of an Art Deco masterpiece

Built by the architect Lucien Pollet and opened in 1929, this public swimming-pool complex became the fashionable place to be throughout the 1930s for anybody wanting to take a dip. It was renowned for its stunning Art Deco design and, perhaps more famously, as the site of the first public appearance of the bikini in 1946. In 1989 the 'white liner', as it was dubbed, was suddenly closed, deemed to be dilapidated and unhygienic.

Renovations were set to cost a fortune and at one point the pool was fated to be destroyed. Supporters fought to save the cherished pool and, although the Culture Minister Jack Lang eventually granted it historical monument status, the complex was abandoned to squatters and graffiti artists until 2012, when private investors took on the cost of an €80 million refurbishment.

The Piscine Molitor was reopened in 2014 to great fanfare. There are two pools, as per its original design – a covered one for the winter and an open-air one for the summer (although both are heated and open all year round). The building's façade and the two pools have been reconstructed in the original style; the railings and stained glass windows are the originals.

Despite the fact that a treasured and beautiful city monument has been restored, Molitor's reopening has been surrounded with controversy. From its humble beginnings as municipal baths, Molitor has become a playground for the wealthy and privileged. Entry is now restricted to a fortunate few – the entrance fee is the price of a night at the five-star hotel, or membership of the exclusive club, which is limited to 1,000 members.

When the pool closed in 1989, it became a canvas for graffiti artists and an attractive venue for skateboarders and ravers. Now only guests of the hotel and exclusive club members are able to enjoy its gleaming new interior.

# SOUTH PIGALLE (SOPI)
Grit, grunge and glamour

For visitors, Pigalle metro station is generally renowned as the alighting point for the Moulin Rouge Cabaret, the Sacré Cœur and the hill that climbs up to Montmartre. That's if they head north. But follow the style-conscious Parisians leaving the station down the hill, and the tourists would encounter a very different neighbourhood: the fashionable South Pigalle – complete with its somewhat affected anglophone nickname, 'SoPi'.

Once dominated by sex shops, massage parlours and prostitutes, the area has been transformed. It now hums with chic cocktail bars, gourmet food shops and stylish restaurants, from sleek speakeasies to brash American-style barbecue shacks, to a kitsch tiki bar housed in a former brothel. As with all hipster haunts, SoPi is a carefully construed mash-up of grit, grunge and glamour, or, as it might otherwise be described, an epitome of absolute gentrification.

A collection of design and vintage boutiques has earned the area a reputation as one of the best for unearthing niche Parisian brands. And its design credentials have been added to by others in the fashion world – Jean Paul Gaultier (b. 1952) used to live here, and Stéphane Ashpool (b. 1982), one of the area's earliest adopters, designed a sweatshirt emblazoned with the word 'Pigalle', which soon attracted partnerships with brands such as Nike. The quirky boutique L'Oeuf, set just off the area's epicentre, rue des Martyrs, further embedded the area's nickname when it debuted a range of SoPi-branded clothing and children's toys.

Just behind the rue des Martyrs is the leafy Place Gustave Toudouze, the heart of the SoPi neighbourhood, where the popular café terraces hum with life whatever the weather and at all times of day. The quirky concept store L'Oeuf (below) offers a fun slice of respite in an area largely dominated by fashionable designer clothes boutiques.

# MAMA SHELTER PARIS
Surprising, streetwise and inventive

In a city where 'chic' and 'style' generally come with a high price tag, the Mama Shelter hotel, designed by Philippe Starck (b. 1949) in 2008, offers a refreshing paradox. Now a small chain of boutique hotels, Mama Shelter builds on the concept Starck launched in New York in 1988 with his achingly trendy Royalton Hotel – cheap chic within a sleek, urban 'design' setting.

Mama Shelter likes things simple, honest and a little bit hip, affirms its website. Rooms have all the latest über-cool technical gadgets, but these sit alongside Starck's trademark quirky touches – provocative quotes on the walls, ceilings and carpets, Batman masks and other cartoon characters on lampshades – and, perhaps the most surprising, a microwave in each room.

Architect Roland Castro (b. 1940) – renowned for his fierce belief in the social role architecture plays in a city – chose a multistorey car park in the ungentrified 20th arrondissement as the site of the hotel. Its interior design continues this rejection of cliché – the ceiling in the bar is covered in graffiti, a reflection of the countless tags that brighten the area and, in keeping with its communitarian spirit, there is no room service.

Mama Shelter is a bold statement of everything a new, 'modern' hotel can be; hotel life reinvented as urban life, in a desirable, aspirational, yet affordable way.

The hotel's bar and restaurant is a fashionable destination in its own right, where diners can also enjoy the Starckian sense of humour and sleek design.

# THE CANOPY, LES HALLES
Sheltered by a vast undulating umbrella

Paris has never fully recovered from the brazen razing in the 1970s of the magnificent, 19 wrought-iron market pavilions at Les Halles, designed by the architect Victor Baltard (1805–74). The complex, an oppressive underground shopping centre and Europe's largest transport hub, erected in their place was considered so unappealing and difficult to navigate that Parisians kept their distance from this national embarrassment. So the unveiling, in 2016, of the city's €1 billion refurbishment project and attempt at making amends was greatly anticipated and, inevitably, heavily scrutinized – not least because of its huge cost and troubled gestation.

The layered roof requires 7,000 tons of steel to hold up the 18,000 pieces of glass that form the 'canopy'.

The first proposal for a simple series of covered lawns was slated by *The New York Times* as too banal, and consequently abandoned. Mayor Bertrand Delanoë's second competition seeking 'an artwork of the 21st century', was won by architects Patrick Berger (b. 1947) and Jacques Anziutti. What appeared, eight years later, was a completely revamped Les Halles, crowned with a giant, undulating glass roof with steel ribs, known as 'the Canopy'. Spanning 2.5 hectares (6 acres), it was designed to open up a new panorama across the city centre. Berger and Anziutti wanted their building to feel like walking into a forest glade, bathed in warm light.

There has, of course, been outrage from some quarters – the colour, form and feeling of the building have been lambasted by many Parisians – but regardless of one's opinion on what is undoubtedly a controversial structure, one has to hope that the intent at the heart of the project prevails. For beyond the consumerism and modernity lies an important cultural focus: a new library, a music and arts conservatory, and a centre for hip-hop will all form part of the complex. Many visitors come from the Parisian suburbs, where French hip hop originated, and Les Halles has consequently been a site of spontaneous street dance. It is hoped that the recording and dance studios and arts facilities available for amateurs will allow this tradition to continue.

# INDEX

# PICTURE CREDITS

# CREDITS

An Hachette UK Company
www.hachette.co.uk

First published in
Great Britain in 2017
by Conran Octopus,
a division of Octopus
Publishing Group Ltd
in conjunction with
the Design Museum

Octopus Publishing
Group Ltd
Carmelite House
50 Victoria Embankment
London EC4Y 0DZ
www.octopusbooks.co.uk
www.octopusbooksusa.com

Distributed in the US by
Hachette Book Group
1290 Avenue of the
Americas, 4th and 5th Floors,
New York, NY 10020

Distributed in Canada by
Canadian Manda Group
664 Annette St., Toronto,
Ontario, Canada  M6S 2C8

Brigitte Fitoussi and
Imogen Fortes assert the
moral right to be identified as
the authors of this work.

A CIP catalogue record
for this book is available
from the British Library.

*Icons selected by:*
Brigitte Fitoussi
*Text written by:*
Brigitte Fitoussi and
Imogen Fortes

*Commissioning Editor:*
Joe Cottington
*Consultant Editor:*
Deyan Sudjic
*Senior Editor:*
Pauline Bache
*Copy Editor:*
Jane Birch
*Design:*
Untitled
*Picture Researcher:*
Claire Gouldstone
*Senior Production Controller:*
Allison Gonsalves

Based on a concept by
Hugh Devlin

Printed and bound in China
ISBN 978 1 84091 742 0

10 9 8 7 6 5 4 3 2 1

The Design Museum is one of the world's
leading museums of contemporary design.
Design Museum Members enjoy free unlimited
entry to the museum's outstanding exhibitions
as well as access to events, tours and
discounts. Becoming a Member is an inspiring
way to support the museum's work.
Visit designmuseum.org/become-a-member
and get involved today.